ROUND
and
SQUARE

by Miriam Schlein

illustrated by Linda Bronson

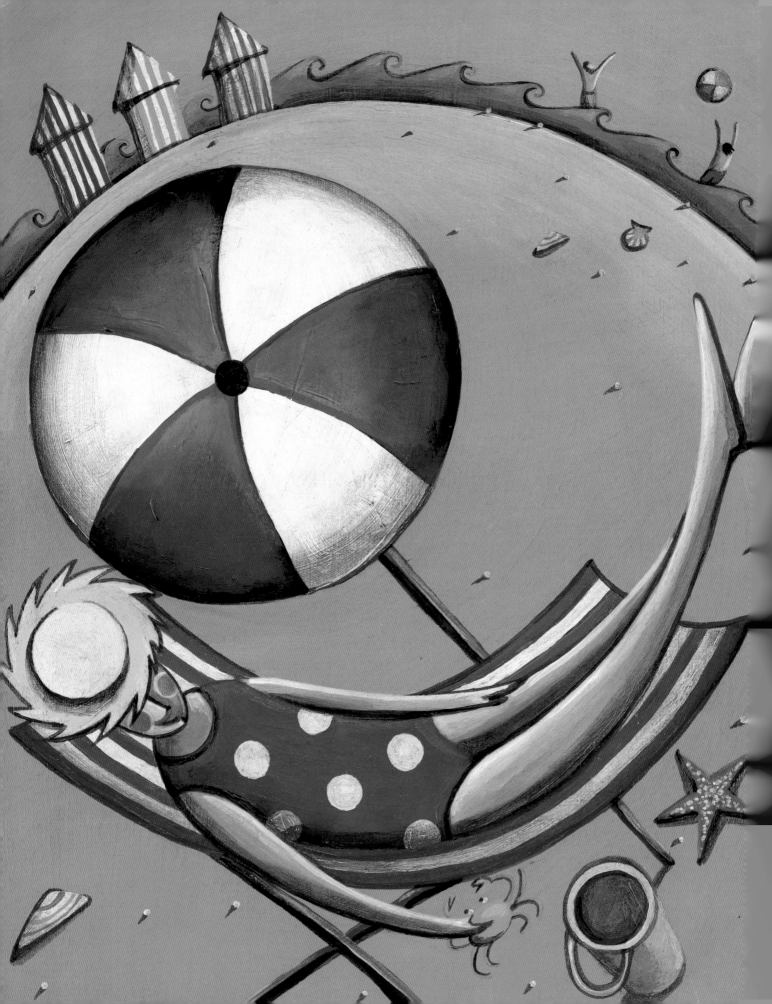

Round, round, fat and round,
so many things in the world are round.

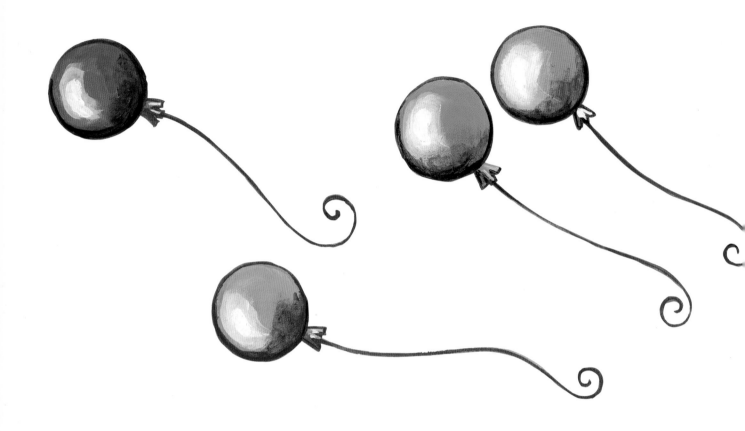

The setting sun,
the rising moon,
a fat balloon,
if it's blue or maroon,
is round, round as a ball.

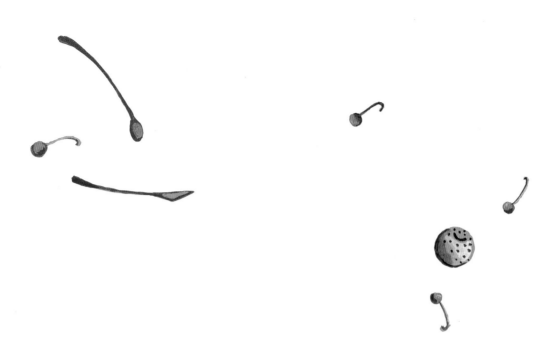

A plate is round.
The world is round,
round as a ball
that rolls down the hall.

A button is round.
And a merry-go-round
goes round in a circle, too.
What else do you know
that is round?

Think of a wheel.
A wheel is a wheel,
and a wheel is always round.

A bicycle wheel
and a wheelbarrow wheel
and every wheel
on an automobile
must always be round.
It can never be square,
or you would never be able
to get anywhere.

You can see a square
almost anywhere.
A book can be square.
A box can be square.
My room is square.
Is yours?
What else can you see
that is square?

Is a bear
or a pear
or a hare
a square?

No, no. A bear is not a square.
Neither is a pear
or a hare
or a fox in its lair.

A fish in the sea
or a bird in the air
can never, no never,
no never be square.

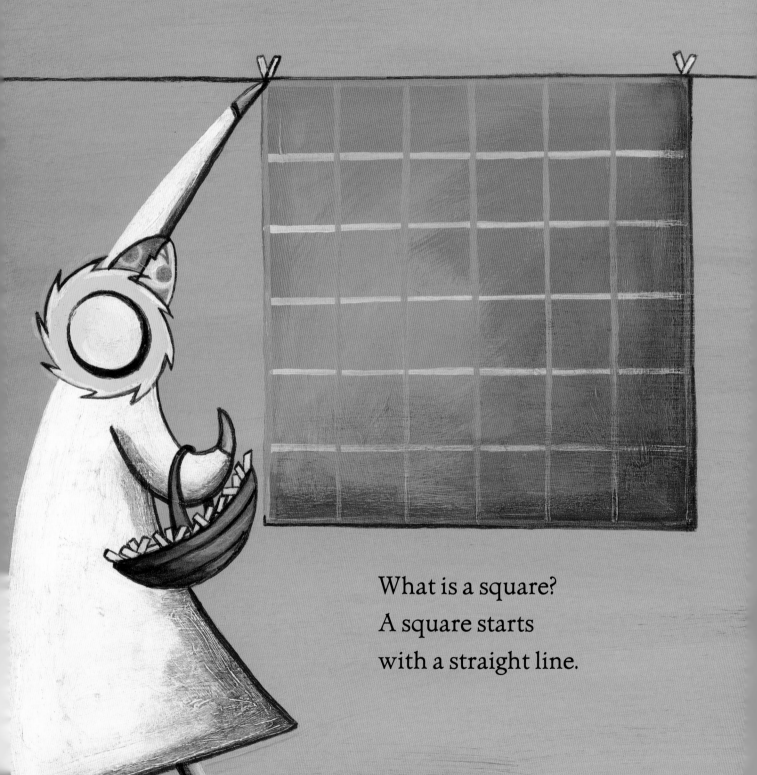

What is a square?
A square starts
with a straight line.

A straight line is a line
that doesn't curve
and doesn't bend.
It can have an end,
but it just can't bend.

If it did, it wouldn't be straight.
It would be a bent line,
or a curvy line.
It would twist and curve
like a crocodile's tail,
and would never, no never,
no never be straight.

Take a ruler.
Draw a straight line.
Is it straight,
straight as can be?

Draw another line.
Draw one more,
and one more.
Now you have a square.

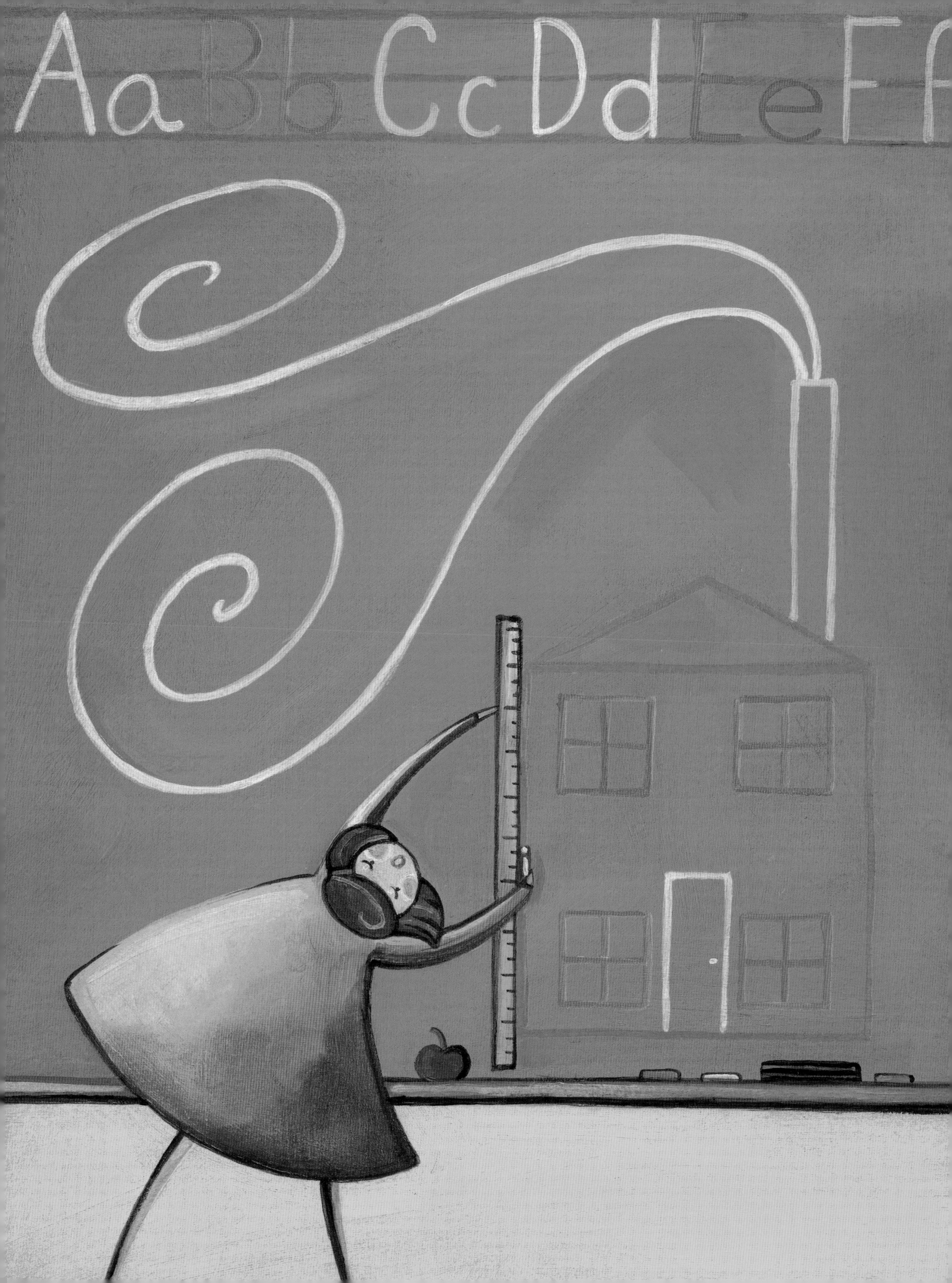
Aa Bb Cc Dd Ee Ff

Look at the bear
and the hare
and the fox in its lair.
They are not round, are they?
And they can never, no never,
no never be square.

But the kitten all curled up
is almost as round as a ball.

And a puppy
begging for food
can sit up straight,
very straight,
almost as straight
as a flagpole.

Look at the giraffe
with its long, tall neck.
It is almost as straight as can be.

And look at the monkey's tail
when it wraps it around a tree.
What kind of shape
do you think it makes?
It looks almost round to me.

But . . .
no boy or girl,
or woman or man,
or fish in the water,
or beast on the land,
or bird in the air,
is ever *exactly* round or square.

Wiggly woggly,
here and there,
everything isn't round or square.
Bumpy lumpy,
zig and zag,
what other kinds of shapes are there?

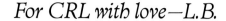

For CRL with love—L.B.

The illustrations for this book were done in acrylic and oil.
The text type is Administer.

Text copyright © 1999, 1952 by Miriam Schlein
Illustrations copyright © 1999 by Linda Bronson

For information contact:
MONDO Publishing
One Plaza Road
Greenvale, New York 11548

MONDO is a registered trademark of Mondo Publishing

Visit our web site at http://www.mondopub.com

Printed in Hong Kong
99 00 01 02 03 04 05 06 07   HC   9 8 7 6 5 4 3 2 1
99 00 01 02 03 04 05 06 07   PB   9 8 7 6 5 4 3 2 1

Designed by Edward Miller
Production by The Kids at Our House

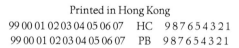

Library of Congress Cataloging-in-Publication Data
Schlein, Miriam.
Round and square / by Miriam Schlein ; illustrated by Linda Bronson.
p. cm.
Summary: Rhyming text examines the basic shapes round and square and how
they appear in things around us, concluding with the recognition that there are
many other shapes in the world as well.
ISBN 1-57255-719-2 (hard : alk. paper). – ISBN 1-57255-720-6
(pbk. : alk. paper)
1. Circle–Juvenile literature. 2. Square–Juvenile literature.
[1. Circle. 2. Square. 3. Shape.] I. Bronson, Linda, ill.
II. Title.
QA484.S34 1999
516'.15–dc21   99-12093
CIP